Dinosaur
DICTIONARY

An A to Z of Dinosaurs and Prehistoric Reptiles

Author Rupert Matthews
Managing Editor Jenny Fry
Managing Art Editor Alix Wood
Production Nicolette Colborne
Illustrators Mike Atkinson, Barry Croucher (Wildlife Art),
Phil Hood (Wildlife Art), Mike Iley (Wildlife Art), Graham Kennedy (Allied),
Martin Knowelden (Virgil Pomfret), Roger Payne (Linden Artists),
Clive Pritchard, Elizabeth Sawyer, Chris Shields, Treve Tamblin (JMA),
Mike Taylor (SGA), Lee Thackray, Phil Weare (Linden Artists),
Christian Webb (Temple Rogers), Steve Weston (Linden Artists).

Planned and produced by
Andromeda Oxford Limited
11-13 The Vineyard
Abingdon
Oxon
OX14 3PX
United Kingdom
www.andromeda.co.uk

This edition produced in 2001 for Scholastic Inc.
Published by Tangerine Press™, an imprint of Scholastic Inc.
555 Broadway,
New York,
NY 10012.

Scholastic and Tangerine Press™ and associated logos
are trademarks of Scholastic Inc.

ISBN 0-439-26471-5

Printed in Spain by Book Print S. L., Barcelona.

Dinosaur
DICTIONARY

An A to Z of Dinosaurs and Prehistoric Reptiles

tangerine
Press™

What is a Dinosaur?

For more than 140 million years dinosaurs were the dominant form of life on Earth, evolving into many shapes and sizes. They died out in a "mass extinction" some 64 million years ago, along with many other types of animals.

Dinosaurs were reptiles that belonged to the diapsid group, meaning they had two openings in the skull bones behind the eye. Modern reptiles are also diapsids, but dinosaurs were different because their legs were held directly under the body, like those of modern mammals. This meant they could move fast, giving them a huge advantage over other animals of the time.

Dinosaurs lived in the Mesozoic Era, which lasted from 225 to 64 million years ago (mya). The Mesozoic is divided into three periods: the Triassic (225-190 mya), the Jurassic (190-135 mya), and the Cretaceous (135-64 mya).

FACT...FACT...FACT

There are two major groups of dinosaurs. Saurischian dinosaurs had hips shaped like those of modern lizards. Saurischian dinosaurs included all meat-eating dinosaurs and sauropods. Ornithischian dinosaurs had hips shaped like those of modern birds. All plant-eating dinosaurs, except sauropods, were ornithischians.

Saurischian hipbone

Ornithischian hipbone

These all belong to the dinosaur group (an example for each group is shown in brackets):

Ankylosaurs
(*Ankylosaurus*)

Coelurosaurs
(*Coelophysis*)

Dromaeosaurs
(*Deinonychus*)

Sauropods
(*Diplodocus*)

Iguanodontids
(*Iguanodon*)

Hadrosaurs
(*Lambeosaurus*)

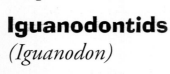
Pachycephalosaurs
(*Pachycephalosaurus*)

Ornithomimids
(*Gallimimus*)

Hypsilophodontids
(*Hypsilophodon*)

Ceratopsians (long-frilled)
(*Pentaceratops*)

Ceratopsians (short-frilled)
(*Centrosaurus*)

Carnosaurs
(*Tyrannosaurus*)

Theropods
(*Baryonyx*)

Fabrosaurids
(*Fabrosaurus*)

Stegosaurs
(*Stegosaurus*)

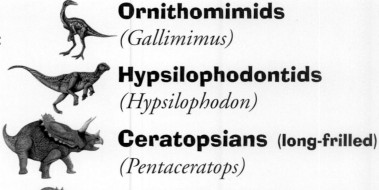

What is not a Dinosaur?

Dinosaurs were not the only types of animals living in the Mesozoic Era. The sky, sea, and land were filled with other types of prehistoric reptiles. The skies were ruled by pterosaurs—which were closely related to dinosaurs. These creatures had wings made of leathery skin, similar to modern bats. From the mid-Jurassic Period onwards there was also an increasing number of birds. In the oceans were plesiosaurs, ichthyosaurs, pliosaurs, and placodonts, as well as turtles, which have survived to modern times. On the land were thecodont and pelycosaur reptiles, as well as lizards and a small number of mammals.

These groups are not dinosaurs, but they lived at the same time as the dinosaurs:

Birds
(Archaeopteryx)

Pelycosaurs
(Dimetrodon)

Plesiosaurs
(Elasmosaurus)

Ichthyosaurs
(Ichthyosaur)

Pterosaurs
(Pterodactylus)

Lizards
(Tanystropheus)

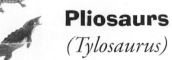
Pliosaurs
(Tylosaurus)

Turtles
(Archelon)

Thecodonts
(Euparkeria)

Placodonts
(Placodus)

FACT...FACT...FACT

Scientists learn about ancient animals from the discovery of fossilized bones and other remains. For a fossil to form after an animal dies, its body must be covered quickly in sand or mud, possibly in a flood. After millions of years the sand turns to sandstone and the bones slowly dissolve and are replaced by minerals, fossilizing them. The minerals can be as hard and heavy as rock. Finally, if the sandstone is worn away, the fossilized bones may be exposed at the Earth's surface allowing scientists the chance to discover them. Scientists carefully dig out the bones and then reassemble them into a complete skeleton.

Most animals are not fossilized. Their bodies are usually eaten by other animals or they rot away. Even those that are fossilized may never be found. Some are destroyed by Earth movements and others remain buried deep below the surface.

The Age of the Dinosaurs

Earth formed from a mass of gas about 4,600 million years ago, and life first appeared on our planet about 600 million years ago. The history of life on Earth has been divided into twelve periods, each lasting several millions of years.

The dinosaurs and other prehistoric reptiles in this book lived during four of these periods, as shown below. Three of these periods of Earth, the Triassic, Jurassic, and Cretaceous Periods, are grouped together in the Mesozoic Era, meaning the Middle Life Era—this is often called the Age of the Dinosaurs. At the end of the Cretaceous Period, all dinosaurs became extinct and their place as the largest land animals was taken by mammals.

Permian 286-225 million years ago ⟶ Triassic 225-190 million years ago ⟶

Cretaceous 135-64 million years ago ⟵ Jurassic 190-135 million years ago ⟵

Evolution

Over a very long period of time one type of animal will change into another. This process is called evolution. The changes may occur for many reasons, but usually they are in response to changes in the environment. For example, if dense forests disappear and are replaced by grassy plains, the animals that once ate leaves may evolve into different animals, with teeth and stomachs able to cope with eating grass. Some animals may not evolve, instead they die out because they cannot cope with the changes.

The small, two-legged Leptoceratops *(top) evolved into the heavier, four-legged* Protoceratops, *which evolved into the horned giants* Chasmosaurus *and* Pentaceratops.

The ages of the Earth

Era	Period	million years ago
Palaeozoic	Precambrian	4600-590
	Cambrian	590-505
	Ordovician	505-440
	Silurian	440-408
	Devonian	408-360
	Carboniferous	360-286
	Permian	286-225
Mesozoic	Triassic	225-190
	Jurassic	190-135
	Cretaceous	135-64
Cenozoic	Palaeocene	64-58
	Eocene	58-37
	Oligocene	37-24
	Miocene	24-5
	Pliocene	5-2
	Pleistocene	2-0

150 million years ago

Earth today

Drifting continents

During the age of the dinosaurs the world looked very different to how it looks today. When dinosaurs first evolved, all the continents of the Earth were joined together in one giant landmass. However, over a period of millions of years, the continents have been slowly drifting apart, causing earthquakes and building mountain ranges where they collide. By the end of the dinosaurs' reign, the world looked fairly similar to how it looks today.

Aa

Alamosaurus
(AL-ah-mo-SORE-us)

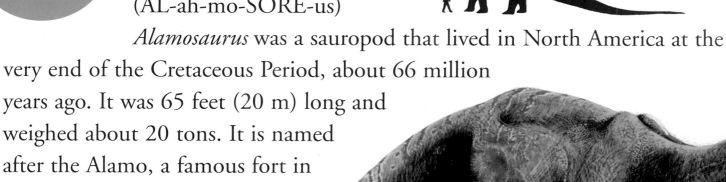

Alamosaurus was a sauropod that lived in North America at the very end of the Cretaceous Period, about 66 million years ago. It was 65 feet (20 m) long and weighed about 20 tons. It is named after the Alamo, a famous fort in Texas, where an important battle took place in 1836.

Albertosaurus
(al-BERT-oh-SORE-us)

Albertosaurus was a large meat-eating dinosaur closely related to the *Tyrannosaurus*. It was only half the size of *Tyrannosaurus*, being about 26 feet (8 m) long and weighing about 2 tons. *Albertosaurus* was numerous in North America 66 million years ago, and many fossils have been found. It may have hunted hadrosaur dinosaurs, killing them with a massive bite to the neck. Its teeth and jaws were very strong, perhaps to crush the neck bones of prey. *Albertosaurus* is named after Alberta, the part of Canada where its fossils were first found.

Ankylosaurus

(ANK-EE-low-SAW-rus)

This dinosaur is often likened to a tank! It had massive bone armor across its back and along its tail, even covering the top of its head. Its sides were protected by sharp spikes, and its tail ended in a massive bone club that could be used to smash any hunter daring to attack it. *Ankylosaurus* had weak teeth, so it may have eaten fruit. It lived in North America at the end of the Cretaceous Period.

Anurognathus

(ann-YOUR-rog-NAY-thus)

This small pterosaur was very acrobatic in the air. It could twist and turn quickly to catch insects in its short, deep jaws. Its small tail and body would have helped it change direction quickly, while its neck could move its head around in search of prey. *Anurognathus* had strong, peglike teeth to crush and grind its food. It lived in central Europe toward the end of the Jurassic Period.

FACT...FACT...FACT

Early flying reptiles, such as *Anurognathus*, had tails and are known as rhamphorhynch pterosaurs. The later pterodactyl pterosaurs had no tails, or only small ones.

Aa

Archaeopteryx

(ARK-ay-OP-tear-ix)

Archaeopteryx is the oldest known bird. It lived in central Europe about 150 million years ago. Unlike modern birds, it had teeth, claws on its wings, and a long bony tail. It was about 14 inches (35 cm) long and probably hunted insects in dense forests.

Archelon

(ar-KEE-lon)

Archelon was the largest turtle that ever lived. It was about 13 feet (4 m) long and lived in the shallow seas that covered what is now Kansas and the Dakotas. Unlike modern turtles and tortoises, *Archelon* did not have a heavy shell covering its back and front. Instead it had strong ridges of bone covered in a tough, leathery skin. This made the animal lighter so that it could swim more easily. Its large front flippers powered it through the water, while its small rear limbs were used for steering. It probably ate squid and jellyfish.

FACT...FACT...FACT

Archaeopteryx was unmistakably a bird. Not only did it have feathers, but it also had a wishbone—formed by the two collarbones joining together. No other type of animal has these features. However, it is also very much like the coelurosaur dinosaurs. In fact, one fossil of *Archaeopteryx* was classified as a *Compsognathus* dinosaur for years, until traces of its feathers were noticed.

Most scientists now believe that these birds are descended from the coelurosaurs, though a few still think they may have descended from pre-dinosaur reptiles. Some experts think the similarities between birds and dinosaurs are so strong that they should be put together in one large group. This would mean that the dinosaurs never really became extinct—they still exist today, as birds!

Barapasaurus (ba-RAP-a-SORE-us)

Barapasaurus was one of the very first sauropods, living about 170 million years ago. Although it was an early sauropod, it was already large, measuring 60 feet (18 m) in length. The name of this dinosaur means "big-leg reptile." Fossils of this sauropod have been found in India.

Baryonyx (BAR-EE-on-ix)

Baryonyx was a meat-eating dinosaur that may have hunted fish! Its large claw could have been used to hook fish out of the water and into its jaws, which were lined with dozens of small, sharp teeth—just right for gripping a slippery fish.

FACT...FACT...FACT

The massive, curved claw of *Baryonyx* was the first part of this dinosaur to be found. The claw was 14 inches (35 cm) long and very sharp. The name *Baryonyx* means "heavy claw."

Bb

Brachiosaurus
(BRACK-ee-oh-SORE-us)

Unlike most sauropods, the front legs of *Brachiosaurus* were longer than its hind legs. It is thought that this was so it could reach high into the treetops to eat leaves other dinosaurs could not reach. *Brachiosaurus* was about 75 feet (23 m) long and weighed about 80 tons.

FACT...FACT...

The skeleton of *Brachiosaurus*, displayed in Berlin, Germany, is the largest complete dinosaur skeleton ever found. It was discovered in Tanzania in 1908 and took months to dig up.

Bradysaurus
(BRAY-dee-SORE-us)

The plant-eating reptile *Bradysaurus* lived in southern Africa in the late Permian Period, about 260 million years ago. It was heavy and short, with legs sprawling from the sides of its body. It measured about 8 feet (2.5 m) long.

Camarasaurus

(KAM-a-ra-SORE-us)

This sauropod dinosaur lived across North America in the late Jurassic Period. Unlike most sauropods, it had teeth that pointed forward and were shaped like spoons with sharp edges. It is thought that its teeth may have been specialized for tearing great mouthfuls of tough ferns and pine needles.

Carcharodontosaurus

(kar-KAR-oh-DONT-oh-SORE-us)

This powerful hunter was about 26 feet (8 m) long, and it lived about 110 million years ago in North Africa. It may have kicked its prey with its hind legs to disable them. Only a few bones of this dinosaur have been found, but enough have been unearthed to put together what it would have looked like.

Cc

Centrosaurus

(SENT-row-SORE-us)

This ceratopsian had a single large horn growing from its nose. The horn was probably used to defend the animal against hunters. It could turn its massive head quickly and easily to face any danger. It may then have charged forward, like a rhinoceros, to drive away attackers.

FACT...FACT...FACT

The skull of *Centrosaurus* shows the sharp teeth that were powered by strong jaw muscles, which ran from the back of its frill down to its lower jaw.

Ceratosaurus

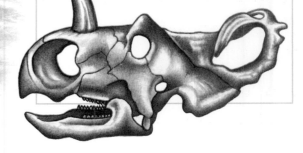

(SIR-a-toe-SORE-us)

This powerful hunter was about 20 feet (6 m) long. It had strong hind legs, which it may have used to kick with, and sharp claws on its front legs to grab hold of prey. Its teeth were sharp and curved, to tear off big chunks of meat. The short horn on its nose may have been used for display purposes, since it was not sharp enough to be used as a weapon.

Cetiosaurus (SEE-tee-oh-SORE-us)

This was one of the first sauropods to be discovered. Scientists were so impressed by its size that they called it *Cetiosaurus,* meaning "whale reptile." It was 60 feet (18 m) long and lived across Europe and North Africa about 160 million years ago. One of the earliest sauropods, *Cetiosaurus* was massively built, but with a shorter neck and tail compared with later sauropods.

Champsosaurus
(KAMP-so-SORE-us)

This 5-foot (1.5-m) -long reptile lived in the rivers and swamps of Europe 75 million years ago. Its long, narrow jaws were filled with dozens of small, sharp teeth, so it probably ate fish. Although it looks similar to a modern crocodile, it is not related. It belonged to a group of reptiles called choristodera, which became extinct 10 million years after the dinosaurs died out.

Cc Chasmosaurus (KAZ-mo-SORE-us)

The horned dinosaurs are divided into two groups, long-frilled and short-frilled. *Chasmosaurus* was a typical member of the long-frilled group. It had a very long, bony frill at the back of its narrow skull, with large holes to reduce the weight. The frill would have been covered in tough, leathery skin and was there as a warning to frighten off attackers. *Chasmosaurus* was about 16 feet (5 m) long and lived in North America 70 million years ago.

Coelophysis

(SEEL-oh-FYE-sis)

Coelophysis was one of the first dinosaurs. It was 10 feet (3 m) long and lived in North America about 220 million years ago. It was a small, fast hunter that preyed on lizards and other small creatures. *Coelophysis* may also have run in packs, hunting larger animals.

Coelurosauravus

(SEEL-your-oh-SORE-ave-us)

This peculiar reptile lived about 260 million years ago in Madagascar. Its "wings" were formed from flaps of skin stretched over bony spines growing out from its ribs. *Coelurosauravus* could not flap its wings, but it did use them to glide from tree to tree, possibly to escape when a hunter approached. It probably hunted insects with its sharp, short teeth.

Compsognathus (komp-SOG-nay-thus)

This tiny dinosaur was no bigger than a modern chicken. It was able to run very quickly and could change direction suddenly to catch the insects and lizards on which it fed. It was probably closely related to *Archaeopteryx*, the first bird—both creatures lived in the wooded islands and lagoons of southern Germany about 130 million years ago.

FACT...FACT...FACT

The name *Compsognathus* means "pretty jaw." Most dinosaurs have names taken from Latin or ancient Greek, though some are named after the place where they were found. The word "saurus," for instance, is Latin for "reptile."

Cc

Corythosaurus

(koe-RITH-oh-SORE-us)

Corythosaurus was one of the largest of the hadrosaurs—the duck-billed dinosaurs. It was 33 feet (10 m) long and lived in North America about 75 million years ago. Like other duck-billed dinosaurs, it had a flat, toothless beak which it used to nip leaves off plants. The leaves were ground up by several rows of teeth at the back of its mouth before being swallowed. *Corythosaurus* may have spent some time in water, as it had webbed fingers and a tail designed for swimming.

The name Corythosaurus *means "helmet reptile" and refers to the odd shape of the skull.*

Cryptocleidus

(KRIP-toe-KLY-duss)

This sea reptile was about 13 feet (4 m) long and lived in a shallow sea that covered Britain about 130 million years ago. It used its flexible neck to move its head around and snap up shrimp and small fish.

Deinocheirus

(DYE-no-KYE-rus)
Nobody really knows what *Deinocheirus* looked like. So far, scientists have found only a gigantic pair of fossilized arms, discovered in the Gobi Desert. Each arm is 8 feet (2.5 m) long and ends in three razor-sharp claws about 10 inches (25 cm) long.

Deinonychus (DYE-no-NYE-kus)

Deinonychus (above) was an active and successful hunter. It could run very quickly, catching prey in its strong hands. It would then kick the victim with its hind legs, inflicting terrible wounds with its long claws. This dinosaur was only about 10 feet (3 m) long, but with its impressive weapons it was able to hunt plant-eaters larger than itself, especially when it hunted in pairs or in packs.

Denversaurus

(DEN-ver-SORE-us)

Denversaurus was about 13 feet (4 m) long and was covered in bony armor. It is named after Denver, Colorado, where its fossils were found. It is one of a group of dinosaurs known as nodosaurids, which had bony plates of armor and long, sharp spikes growing from their bodies. Unfortunately, very few fossils of these dinosaurs have been found, so scientists still have a lot to learn about them.

Dd Dicraeosaurus

(dye-KRAY-oh-SORE-us)

Dicraeosaurus was closely related to *Diplodocus*, but was much shorter at just 39 feet (12 m) long. It lived 130 million years ago in East Africa. Its name means "forked reptile" and refers to the odd shape of the bones in its tail and back. Each spine was forked at the top, like a Y-shaped prong sticking upwards.

Dicynodon (dye-SINE-oh-don)

This reptile lived about 260 million years ago in southern Africa. *Dicynodon* means "two dog tooth" and refers to this creature's powerful tusks. Besides these, however, the creature had almost no teeth. It may have used the tusks to dig up juicy roots, which it could then mash up and swallow.

Dimetrodon

(dye-MEE-troe-don)

Dimetrodon may have used the large "sail" on its back to absorb the warm rays of the sun early in the morning. The sail would have absorbed heat and warmed the reptile's blood. It could then become active and begin its daily hunt for food. It lived in North America some 270 million years ago.

Dimorphodon

(dye-MORF-oh-DON)

This flying reptile had a very large, deep head, with thick, colorful jaws. Its head was an unusual puffinlike shape, almost like a beak. Its brightly colored jaws were probably used for display purposes. Unlike most pterosaurs, *Dimorphodon* could walk fairly well, scampering along the ground on its hind legs.

Dd

Diplodocus
(dip-LOD-oh-kus)

Diplodocus was one of the great plant-eating dinosaurs of the late Jurassic Period. This enormous dinosaur measured 100 feet (30 m) in length. Most of its length was made up of its long neck and extra-long tail. The bones in its neck and tail were hollowed out so that only a series of struts remained. This meant that *Diplodocus* was very light for its size—about 10 tons. It used its long neck to move its tiny head around in search of food. It ate leaves, then swallowed stones to grind them to a pulp in its stomach.

The spines over the hips supported muscles that may have allowed Diplodocus *to rear up on its hind legs to reach high into the trees and feed on their leaves.*

FACT...FACT...FACT

Diplodocus had very few enemies, mainly because of its enormous size. However, if it was attacked it could have used its long, flexible tail as a weapon. The whiplike tip would easily have stunned a predator.

Edaphosaurus (ee-DAFF-oh-SORE-us)

This 10-foot (3-m) reptile from central Europe lived about 280 million years ago. *Edaphosaurus* had a mouthful of teeth! In addition to closely packed peglike teeth lining its jaws, it also had teeth on the roof of its mouth. The teeth ground down plant food before it passed to its huge gut, which took up much of its body. The large "sail" on its back may have been used to absorb heat from the sun, but some scientists think it was a brightly colored display, something like a peacock's tail.

Edmontosaurus

(ed-MON-to-SORE-us)

This hadrosaur is named after the Canadian city of Edmonton, near where fossils of it were found. It was 43 feet (13 m) long and lived about 70 million years ago. This dinosaur had an astonishing 1,000 teeth in its mouth! These were arranged in several rows on either side of its jaws so that tough plant food could be ground to a pulp before it was swallowed.

FACT...FACT...FACT

Hadrosaur dinosaurs lived toward the end of the Cretaceous Period in western North America and eastern Asia, which were then joined together. Although they usually walked on their hind legs, the hadrosaurs could go down on all fours to feed. The front feet were equipped with small hoofs able to take the weight of the animal.

Ee

Elasmosaurus (ee-LAZ-mo-SORE-us)

No less than half of the 46-foot (14-m) length of *Elasmosaurus* was made up of its neck. It is thought that this reptile swam on the water's surface with its head and neck held upright so that it could look for fish or other prey. When a meal was spotted, *Elasmosaurus* would lunge its head forward to grab it. This creature lived 75 million years ago in seas around North America and Asia.

Erythrosuchus

(eh-REE-throw-SOO-kus)

Living 240 million years ago in southern Africa, *Erythrosuchus* was 16 feet (5 m) long and was the largest hunter of its time. Its large head was over 3 feet (1 m) long, and it had strong jaws filled with sharp but fairly simple teeth. Although it was heavy, it could probably move quickly over short distances.

Eudimorphodon

(you-dye-MORF-oh-DON)

Eudimorphodon was one of the first pterosaurs, living about 220 million years ago in southern Europe. Like other pterosaurs, it had a wing made up of leathery skin which stretched between its very long fourth finger and its hind legs. The tail was long and stiff with a flap of skin at the rear, which may have acted like a rudder when flying. It was an active flyer and could flap its wings fairly strongly, though not as well as a modern bird.

Eudimorphodon's front teeth were long and sharp, so it may have swooped low over the sea or lakes to snatch fish from near the surface.

Ee

Euoplocephalus

(you-op-loh-KEFF-ah-lus)

Euoplocephalus was very similar to *Ankylosaurus*, though at 23 feet (7 m) long it was somewhat smaller. Some scientists think the two creatures were really just slightly different versions of the same type of dinosaur. The back and sides of *Euoplocephalus* were covered in thick plates of bony armor. Its head was even more heavily armored. Even its eyelids had bone coverings to protect its eyes from attack.

Euparkeria

(you-par-KIR-ree-ah)

Although it was only about 24 inches (60 cm) long, *Euparkeria* may have been an ancestor of the later dinosaurs. It lived in southern Africa about 240 million years ago. It was an active hunter and could run very quickly on its hind legs for short distances to catch prey. Its jaws were armed with long, sharp teeth which had sawlike edges for gripping struggling prey.

Fabrosaurus

(FAB-roe-SORE-us)

Living 200 million years ago in southern Africa, *Fabrosaurus* was one of the very earliest ornithischian, or bird-hipped, dinosaurs. This group later included the hadrosaurs, stegosaurs, and ceratopsians, but *Fabrosaurus* was typical of the earlier types, such as *Lesothosaurus*. It was just 3 feet (1 m) long and very lightly built. It ran on its hind legs and ate plants with its small, leaf-shaped teeth. Its strong arms may have been used to grab hold of branches while the dinosaur ate the leaves.

Gg Gallimimus

(GAL-ee-MEE-mus)

Gallimimus, which means "chicken mimic," was up to 13 feet (4 m) long and was the largest of the ornithomimid, or bird-mimic, dinosaurs. The ornithomimid family was named because these dinosaurs resembled ostriches with tails, and they could run quickly. *Gallimimus* may have run across open plains in small herds, feeding on insects, fruits, or seeds with their grasping hands.

Gigantosaurus

(JIYE-gant-oh-SORE-us)

This massive meat-eater was even larger than *Tyrannosaurus*. *Gigantosaurus* was 47 feet (14.3 m) long and weighed about 8 tons. It lived in South America about 70 million years ago, but fossils were only discovered in 1995. This mighty dinosaur was an active predator, hunting the very largest animals of its time.

Herrarasaurus (hair-RARE-oh-SORE-us)

Herrarasaurus lived in South America 220 million years ago. It was about 10 feet (3 m) long and weighed just 220 pounds (100 kg). It had a large jaw with sharp, curved teeth and moved on its hind legs. Some scientists think that it may have been the ancestor of the later sauropod giants.

FACT...FACT...FACT

Some skulls belonging to *Heterodontosaurus* have been found without the middle tusklike teeth. The skulls do not even have sockets where the tusks could grow. Some scientists believe these are female skulls. If only males had tusks, they may have used them for fighting each other.

Heterodontosaurus

(HET-err-oh-DON-toh-SORE-us)

This dinosaur's name means "reptile with different types of teeth." *Heterodontosaurus* had three different types of teeth. At the front were small, pointed teeth, behind these were long, sharp, tusklike teeth, and at the back were tall, chisel-like teeth. It is thought the front teeth nipped off leaves, which were then sliced up by the back teeth. The body of *Heterodontosaurus* was very much like that of a fabrosaur. It is thought that *Heterodontosaurus* was also an early ornithischian, or bird-hipped, dinosaur. It lived about 210 million years ago in southern Africa.

Hh

Homalocephale

(HOM-al-oh-KEF-al-ee)

This 10-foot (3-m) -long dinosaur belonged to a family called pachycephalosaurs, all of which had massive plates of bone on the tops of their heads. *Homalocephale* also had bony knobs and pits on its head. It is thought that rival males engaged in ritual head-butting contests to settle disputes. It lived in eastern Asia about 80 million years ago.

Hypacrosaurus

(hip-AH-kro-SORE-us)

This large hadrosaur lived in North America about 70 million years ago and may have been related to *Corythosaurus*. Unlike similar dinosaurs, *Hypacrosaurus* had a thick, fleshy ridge running along its back and tail, which explains its name of "high-ridge reptile."

Hypsilophodon (hip-see-LOAF-oh-don)

This fast-running dinosaur lived in northern Europe about 120 million years ago. When a fossil of *Hypsilophodon* was first found in 1870, scientists believed that its fourth toe pointed backward. Because this could have been used to grasp branches, the dinosaur was thought to be able to climb trees to reach their leaves. However, we now know that its toe pointed forward and that *Hypsilophodon* could not climb trees.

Ichthyosaur

(ICK-thee-oh-SORE)

The name ichthyosaur means "fish reptile." This describes these marine animals very well because, although they are reptiles, they look just like fish! There were many different types of ichthyosaur, ranging in size from 3 to 50 feet (1–15 m). Most ichthyosaurs hunted fish, squid, and other small sea creatures. They died out about 90 million years ago. The ichthyosaur shown is the *Eurhinosaurus*, which had a long, pointed snout studded with teeth.

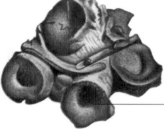

The disk-shaped backbones of ichthyosaurs are often found in rocks from Jurassic times.

Iguanodon

(ig-WAH-no-DON)

Iguanodon was the second dinosaur ever to be found. Fossils were named in 1825, before scientists even knew dinosaurs had existed on Earth! They thought this was a type of giant lizard and sketched pictures of it walking on all fours. We now know this was a 30-foot (9-m) -long, two-legged dinosaur that ate plants, and that it lived in western Europe about 120 million years ago.

Jj

Jenghizkhanosaurus

(jen-giz-KON-oh-SORE-us)

About 70 million years ago this large meat-eater lived in Mongolia. It was similar to the *Tyrannosaurus* of North America, but it was smaller and lighter. It is thought that it could run quickly for short distances and that its jaws were specially strengthened to withstand the force of any impact caused when it sunk its teeth into its prey. It may have hidden in trees waiting for a tasty meal to pass by, and then charged out with its jaws wide open to attack its victim.

FACT...FACT...FACT

This dinosaur used to be thought of as a type of *Tyrannosaurus* called *Tyrannosaurus bataar*. But in 2000 scientists decided that it was so different that it should be given a name of its own. They chose the name of Genghis Khan, a famous ruler of Mongolia, where its fossils were found.

Kannemeyria

(KAN-ee-MAY-er-ee-ah)

Kannemeyria was almost as large as a cow and plodded around southern Africa, South America, and Asia some 240 million years ago. It had unusual jaws that slid backward and forward to help it grind up the leaves that it ate. It belonged to a group of reptiles called therapsids, which had several similarities to mammals. A group of therapsids later evolved into the mammals.

Kentrosaurus

(KEN-troe-SORE-us)

Kentrosaurus was related to *Stegosaurus*, but was much smaller at 16 feet (5 m) long. It ate plants and moved around slowly on its massive legs. If it was attacked, it would turn away from its attacker showing the long, sharp spikes on its back as a form of defense. It may even have pushed itself backward if an enemy got too close, hoping to stab its attacker. *Kentrosaurus* lived in southern Africa about 150 million years ago.

Kk

Kronosaurus (CROW-no-SORE-us)

About 120 million years ago much of Australia was covered by warm, shallow seas. Here lived the mighty *Kronosaurus,* which grew to over 39 feet (12 m) in length. Nearly 10 feet (3 m) of its length was taken up by its massive head. It had strong jaws and sharp teeth to snap up fish and squid.

Kuehneosaurus (qway-nee-oh-SORE-us)

This small lizard lived in Europe in the Triassic Period and grew to a length of 25.5 inches (65 cm). It had very long hind legs, so it may have used them to run quickly over short distances. The "wings" on either side of its body were formed by a flap of skin stretched over greatly lengthened ribs. The "wings" allowed *Kuehneosaurus* to glide through the air.

FACT...FACT...FACT

A gliding lizard may seem odd, but its body form does have advantages—escaping quickly from attackers, or gliding from one tree to another for food. This creature has evolved three different times from three different types of reptile. *Coelurosauravus* lived 260 million years ago, and *Kuehneosaurus* 230 million years ago. Today the Draco flying lizard lives in the forests of Southeast Asia. It also has "wings" formed by rib bones covered in skin. It can glide up to 197 feet (60 m).

Lambeosaurus

(LAM-bee-oh-SORE-us)

At 50 feet (15 m) long, *Lambeosaurus* was one of the largest hadrosaurs. The large crest on its head was hollow and connected to its nostrils. It is thought that *Lambeosaurus* may have used these chambers to make its cries and roars louder, in the way a guitar box boosts the sound of guitar strings. *Lambeosaurus* lived about 80 million years ago in North America.

The skull of Lambeosaurus *had a large crest with a long backward-pointing spike.*

Leptoceratops

(LEP-toe-SER-a-tops)

This curious dinosaur was probably an ancestor of the mighty ceratopsian or horned dinosaurs. It could walk on four legs or run just on its hind legs. The back of its skull extended out in a small frill, which acted as an anchor for its powerful jaw muscles. This frill later developed into the head shields of the ceratopsians. *Leptoceratops* lived in North America and Asia about 90 million years ago.

Mm Maiasaura

(MY-ah-SORE-ra)

The name of this dinosaur means "good mother reptile." It was given to the creature because scientists found its fossilized nests complete with eggs and babies. This showed that *Maiasaura* cared for its young until they were old enough to look after themselves. The parents might have brought mouthfuls of leaves and fruit for the young babies to eat.

Mamenchisaurus

(mah-MEN-key-SORE-us)

The 36-foot (11-m) neck of *Mamenchisaurus* was the longest neck of any creature that has ever lived! It was very stiff, and only the section near the head could be twisted around. *Mamenchisaurus* lived 140 million years ago in eastern Asia and is named after Mamenchi, the Chinese town where its fossils were found.

Massospondylus

(MASS-oh-SPOND-eye-lus)

Massospondylus belonged to the prosauropod group of dinosaurs, the ancestors of the later giant sauropods. It lived about 210 million years ago in southern Africa. It had a tiny head on top of a long, flexible neck and spent most of its time eating.

FACT...FACT...FACT

Prosauropods, like *Massospondylus*, and the later sauropods had the odd habit of swallowing large stones. The stones remained in the dinosaur's stomach and were churned around with food, grinding and thumping tough leaves to a mush. This meant that the dinosaur did not need to chew its food—it just gulped it down—which saved time.

Mastodonsaurus

(MASS-toe-don-SORE-us)

Growing up to 10 feet (3 m) long, *Mastodonsaurus* was the largest amphibian that has ever existed. It lived in central Europe about 220 million years ago, at the same time as the earliest dinosaurs. *Mastodonsaurus* probably lived in swamps and shallow lakes, where it hunted fish.

Mm

Megalosaurus

(MEG-ah-low-SORE-us)

This fearsome hunter was about 26 feet (8 m) long and lived in Europe during the later Jurassic Period, about 150 million years ago. It had a very muscular neck, allowing it to seize struggling prey in its mouth. *Megalosaurus* would also have held its victims in its front claws, while it tore off chunks of meat with its curved teeth.

FACT...FACT...FACT

Megalosaurus was the very first dinosaur to be discovered. The fossils of this dinosaur were found in England in 1824 and studied by the scientist William Buckland. In 1841 the bones were used by Richard Owen to prove that there had been a group of very large reptiles which he named "dinosaurs," meaning "terrible reptiles."

Minmi (min-MEE)

This armored dinosaur was discovered in 1980 and is named after the settlement in Queensland, Australia, where the fossils were found. Scientists do not know very much about *Minmi*, because only parts of the skeleton have been found. It was about 6.5 feet (2 m) long and was covered in bony plates—a defense against attackers.

Moschops

(mosh-OPS)

Moschops was about 16 feet (5 m) long and was massively built, with short, sturdy legs and a deep, heavy body. Its teeth were shaped like chisels, so it probably sliced leaves off plants and swallowed them whole. This creature was not a dinosaur, but may have been related to the therapsid reptiles, which evolved into mammals. *Moschops* lived about 260 million years ago in southern Africa.

Mm

Muttaburrasaurus
(MUTT-ah-BUH-ra-SORE-us)

Muttaburrasaurus was about 23 feet (7 m) long and lived in Australia about 100 million years ago. It was unearthed in 1981 from what are now the grasslands of central Queensland. *Muttaburrasaurus* was closely related to the *Iguanodon* and led a similar life, munching plants and moving around in herds. The unusual crest on its nose was made of solid bone, but nobody knows yet what it was used for.

Mystriosuchus (miss-TREE-oh-SUCH-us)

This early form of crocodile lived in Europe about 180 million years ago. It is thought that the creature spent most of its time in the ocean, where it hunted fish with its long, tooth-studded jaws. *Mystriosuchus* grew to about 13 feet (4 m) long.

Nanotyrannus

(NAN-OH-tir-RAN-us)

This dinosaur has been a puzzle ever since scientists first discovered it in the 1950s. It looks like a small *Tyrannosaurus rex*, and "nano" means "small," but nobody is certain if this was a young *Tyrannosaurus* or a completely different species of small hunter. A *Triceratops* fossil has been found with several broken *Nanotyrannus* teeth embedded in it. There are too many teeth to come from one *Nanotyrannus*, so these small creatures probably hunted in packs.

FACT...FACT...FACT

The dispute about whether *Nanotyrannus* is a young *Tyrannosaurus rex* or a different species centers on its skull. It has a narrow snout and large eyes, and was held more horizontally than in *Tyrannosaurus*. Scientists are now looking for more *Nanotyrannus* fossils to solve the dispute.

The fossilized bones of Nanotyrannus *were found in North America.*

Nothosaurus

(NO-though-SORE-us)

This ocean-dwelling reptile lived around the coasts of Europe and Asia some 220 million years ago. It ate fish, which it caught in its many long teeth. Although it had webbed feet for swimming, its legs were strong enough for *Nothosaurus* to walk on land. It may have gone ashore to lay its eggs.

Oo

Oligokyphus (oh-LIG-oh-KYE-fuss)

Living 170 million years ago in Europe, this was a very advanced type of mammal-like reptile. It had long, strong front teeth, like a modern beaver, so it probably gnawed at tough plant food.

Omeisaurus (OH-MAY-sore-us)

Omeisaurus lived about 150 million years ago. It was named after Mount Omei in China, where its fossils were found in 1939. This sauropod dinosaur had a very long neck. Its nostrils were right at the front of its snout, which is unusual in sauropods—most had nasal openings at the top of their head. Its teeth were fairly weak, so it may have fed on a specialized diet not liked by other dinosaurs, but nobody knows what this might have been.

Ornitholestes (or-NEETH-oh-LESS-tees)

This 6.5-foot (2-m) -long dinosaur had sharp teeth and powerful biting muscles, so it would have been able to attack and kill a number of different animals. Its front legs ended in grasping claws to hold small creatures while it killed them. The name *Ornitholestes* means "bird robber" and was given to this creature because it lived around the same time as the first birds—about 150 million years ago in Europe. It may have been strong and agile enough to capture them.

Ornithomimus

(or-NEETH-oh-ME-mus)

Ornithomimus means "bird mimic." The name was given to this dinosaur because it looked a little like a modern ostrich. It lived about 70 million years ago in North America and may have been one of the very last dinosaurs. It was about 13 feet (4 m) long and was just one of several different types of similar dinosaurs that are called "ostrich dinosaurs."

FACT...FACT...FACT

Scientists still know very little about how the ostrich dinosaurs lived. They were all long-legged sprinters and had front limbs, or "hands," adapted for grasping small objects. Their jaws were beaklike and had no teeth at all—though they may have used them to pick up and eat seeds or fruit. These creatures may have lived in open countryside, where they would have needed to run fast to escape danger. Some scientists think they may have waded in the ocean searching for crabs, shrimps, and other coastal animals.

Oviraptor

(OH-vee-RAP-tore)

The name of this dinosaur means "egg thief." It got its name because the first fossils of *Oviraptor* were found next to the eggs of a horned dinosaur. It is very likely that its powerful, but toothless, jaws would have been useful for cracking open eggs and sucking up their contents. Some types of *Oviraptor* had horns and crests on the tip of their nose. These may have been used for displays.

Pp Pachycephalosaurus (PACK-ee-KEFF-ah-low-SORE-us)

This remarkable dinosaur was about 16 feet (5 m) long and ate plants. The top of its skull was covered with an enormously thick layer of solid bone, together with knobs and studs. It is thought that rival *Pachycephalosaurus* males used their skulls in fights. They may have charged at each other with lowered heads, each trying to butt the other to the ground.

A Pachyrhinosaurus skull showing its rough pad of bone.

Pachyrhinosaurus
(PACK-ee-RYNE-oh-SORE-us)

Pachyrhinosaurus was a horned dinosaur, but without horns! It had a body and skull very much like that of normal horned dinosaurs, such as *Triceratops*, but where the brow horns should have been there was a large, rough pad of bone. Scientists are still not certain what this bone pad may have been used for.

Parasaurolophus

(PA-ra-SORE-OH-loh-fuss)

Measuring 33 feet (10 m) in length, *Parasaurolophus* was one of the largest of the hadrosaur dinosaurs. Like other hadrosaurs, it fed on pine needles and tough plant food, which it stripped off with its broad, toothless snout. It then ground the plants to a pulp with its large, powerful teeth. *Parasaurolophus* lived 70 million years ago in North America. It could walk on all four legs when feeding, but could also run fast on its hind legs when danger threatened.

FACT...FACT...FACT

The long bone crest on the head of *Parasaurolophus* was hollow. The air passages from the nostrils ran up to the top of the crest, then back down again. It is thought that the hollow passages were used to increase the deep, booming calls of these animals.

Pentaceratops

(PENT-ah-SEH-ra-tops)

The name of this dinosaur from 70 million years ago means "five-horned face." When scientists first found a skull belonging to *Pentaceratops* they thought it had five horns. But we now know that it had only three horns. The other two growths were enlarged cheekbones. Like other horned dinosaurs, *Pentaceratops* was a plant-eater.

Peteinsaurus

(PEH-tine-SORE-us)

This small flying reptile lived about 180 million years ago. Like other pterosaurs, it had a furry body and may have been able to generate its own internal heat, which most reptiles cannot do. Its sharp, small teeth show that it probably ate insects, which it caught in flight.

Placodus

(PLACK-oh-dus)

The sea reptile *Placodus* lived about 220 million years ago around the coasts of Europe. Its front teeth were strong and pointed forward, while its back teeth were broad, flat, and very powerful. It is likely that *Placodus* used its front teeth to pluck shellfish off rocks, then crushed them with its back teeth.

Plesiosaurus

(PLEE-see-oh-SORE-us)

Plesiosaurus was about 8 feet (2.5 m) long and lived in the shallow seas that covered western Europe some 180 million years ago. It used the flippers on its body to dart around, quickly changing direction, while its long neck snaked out to grab fish, squid, and other small animals. There were several similar types of sea reptiles, all called plesiosaurs.

FACT...FACT...FACT

Long-necked plesiosaurs fit the descriptions of both ancient sea monsters and creatures like the modern-day smooth-skinned "sea serpent" spotted in Chesapeake Bay in the USA, or the famous "Loch Ness Monster" in Scotland.

Protoceratops

(pro-toe-SER-a-tops)

The name of this dinosaur means "first horned face" because it was one of the earliest of the horned dinosaurs. *Protoceratops* was just 6 feet (1.8 m) long, smaller than the later horned dinosaurs, and it lived about 90 million years ago in eastern Asia. Some nests have been found with fossilized eggs containing unhatched baby *Protoceratops*.

Pp

Psittacosaurus

(SIH-tak-oh-SORE-us)

Psittacosaurus lived some 120 million years ago in eastern Asia. It could walk on all fours or on its hind legs. Its skull was similar to that of the horned dinosaurs—its jaws ended in a deep beak with sharp edges, while the back of the skull had a ridge, like a small frill. Perhaps *Psittacosaurus* was the ancestor of *Protoceratops*.

Pteranodon

(tear-RAN-oh-DON)

Unlike most other flying reptiles, *Pteranodon* had no teeth. It is thought it may have scooped up fish in its jaws and swallowed them whole. It had a wingspan of about 23 feet (7 m). *Pteranodon* lived in Europe and North America about 70 million years ago.

Pterodactylus (TEAR-oh-DAK-til-us)

This small flying reptile had a wingspan of just 27.5 inches (70 cm), but it gave its name to an entire group of flying reptiles. The pterodactyls had very small tails and slender necks. These animals appeared about 140 million years ago and survived right up to the end of the Cretaceous Period.

FACT...FACT...FACT

Because the bones of flying reptiles were very light and fragile, their fossils are rarely found.

Quetzalcoatlus

(KWET-sal-coh-AT-lus)
With a wingspan of 39 feet (12 m) and a weight of 143 pounds (65 kg), *Quetzalcoatlus* was the largest flying animal ever. It probably flew over inland areas, looking for dinosaur carcasses to eat.

Rr

Rhamphorhynchus

(RAM-for-RIN-kus)
Like *Pterodactylus*, this small flying reptile gave its name to a whole group. The rhamphorhyncoids had long tails with a small skin flap at the end that acted as a rudder. They evolved 190 million years ago and became extinct 140 million years ago.

Riojasaurus (REE-OH-ha-SORE-us)

This plant-eating dinosaur lived in South America some 215 million years ago. It was about 33 feet (10 m) long and was one of the largest of the prosauropod dinosaurs. The prosauropods lived before the giant sauropods, which were probably descended from them.

Ss

Saltasaurus
(SALT-ah-SORE-us)

This 39-foot (12-m) -long sauropod dinosaur (below) lived about 80 million years ago, long after most sauropods had died out. It was very unusual in that it had armor made up of thousands of bone studs across its back. Some of these studs carried horny lumps for added protection against attack. Scientists believe that during the mid-Cretaceous Period South America was cut off from all other land, which allowed this odd creature to evolve.

Saurolophus
(SORE-OH-low-fuss)

This hadrosaur dinosaur was about 30 feet (9 m) long and lived in North America 70 million years ago. It is thought that a flap of skin ran from the tip of its snout to the tip of the crest on the top of its head. This skin flap could be blown up to make a honking noise.

Scelidosaurus
(SKELL-id-oh-SORE-us)

Scelidosaurus lived in Britain about 190 million years ago. It had a tiny head with weak jaws and teeth, and a massive body that was covered in bony armor and short spikes. *Scelidosaurus* was one of the earliest of the ornithischian, or bird-hipped, dinosaurs and may have been the ancestor of the later stegosaurs and ankylosaurs.

Segnosaurus

(SEG-no-SORE-us)

This small dinosaur (left) was an unusual meat-eater, as the front of its jaws had a horn beak instead of teeth. Its front legs had three fingers with sharp claws, and its hind feet were sturdy and very wide. It is possible that it had evolved to run on unstable surfaces, such as the desert sand or marshy mud of eastern Asia about 80 million years ago.

Seismosaurus

(SIZE-mo-SORE-us)

Seismosaurus was a huge dinosaur that lived about 150 million years ago in North America. Its name means "earthquake reptile" and was given to it because scientists thought its footsteps must have made the ground shake. It was up to 164 feet (50 m) long and may have weighed 30 tons. The fossils of this mighty beast were found in 1991 and have not yet been fully excavated and studied.

Shunosaurus

(SHOO-no-SORE-us)

The Chinese scientists who dug up this 39-foot (12-m) -long sauropod dinosaur in 1981 got a surprise. Attached to the end of its long tail was a massive bone club. *Shunosaurus* must have used this weapon to fight off attacks from hunting dinosaurs. No other sauropods had tail clubs, so this creature is one of a kind.

Ss

Spinosaurus (SPINE-oh-SORE-us)

Spinosaurus was a 39-foot (12-m) -long hunter from North Africa that lived about 80 million years ago. It had a large sail along its back that was supported by upright bone rods. The rods grew upward from the dinosaur's backbone—the tallest rod was 6.5 feet (2 m) long. The sail may have been used as a display to rival males, or possibly to signal to friendly *Spinosaurus*—nobody is sure. It would, however, have been quite fragile and may have been easily broken in a fight. Perhaps *Spinosaurus* did not actively hunt other dinosaurs, but fed on the bodies of dinosaurs that had already died.

FACT...FACT...FACT

Unlike *Stegoceras*, most of the pachycephalosaurs are known only from their skulls. They may have lived in the hills, where their bodies were not preserved as fossils, but their heavy skulls rolled downhill and were buried in riverbeds.

Stegoceras

(STEG-oh-SER-ass)

The entire 8-foot (2.5-m) -long body of *Stegoceras* was made for head-butting. Its neck, spine, and tail were built so that they would lock in a stiff, straight line when its head was lowered. In this way the crushing blow of two *Stegoceras* hitting each other head-on would be spread through their whole bodies without causing too much damage. The head-butting contests may have been used to settle disputes over feeding grounds or at breeding time.

Stegosaurus (STEG-oh-SORE-us)

Stegosaurus is one of the best-known dinosaurs, thanks to some splendid fossilized skeletons found in North America. It lived about 150 million years ago and was nearly 30 feet (9 m) long. The spikes on the end of its tail would have been swung from side to side to deter attackers. The large bone plates that stuck up along its back may have been a form of protection too, or they may have been covered in a thin layer of skin that could be made to change color as a display.

Stenopterygius (sten-OP-ter-REE-jee-us)

This reptile was so well adapted to life in the ocean that it looked like a fish and could not survive on dry land. Its swimming power came from lashing its tail from side to side, and it used its flippers mainly for steering. Some fossils show babies still inside the bodies of their mothers—this shows us that *Stenopterygius* gave birth to live young rather than laying eggs.

Tt

Talarurus

(TALE-ah-roo-roos)

This 16-foot (5-m) -long ankylosaur dinosaur was almost entirely covered in strong bone armor as a defense against attack. Its tail was equipped with extremely powerful muscles and a large bone club—this was a very dangerous weapon. *Talarurus* could easily break the leg of an attacking hunter when it swung its tail club from side to side.

Tanystropheus

(tan-ee-STROW-fee-us)

This extraordinary lizard lived about 225 million years ago in central Europe and may have been related to the ancestors of the dinosaurs. It was about 10 feet (3 m) long, but half of its length was taken up by its neck. It is thought that this creature may have lived along the coast, using its long neck to dip into the water to snap up fish and shellfish.

Tarbosaurus

(TAR-bow-SORE-us)

The 46-foot (14-m) *Tarbosaurus* lived in central Asia about 80 million years ago. It was very similar to *Tyrannosaurus*, which lived in North America, but it was slightly smaller. *Tarbosaurus* may have been a powerful hunter of the larger plant-eating dinosaurs, or it may have eaten the remains of dinosaurs that had already died.

Titanosaurus (tye-TANN-oh-SORE-us)

Titanosaurus was a 39-foot (12-m) -long sauropod named after the Titans—a race of giants in ancient Greek mythology. *Titanosaurus* was very similar to *Saltasaurus*, but scientists are not certain if it had bony armor like *Saltasaurus*. It lived in India, Hungary, and Argentina about 70 million years ago.

Torosaurus

(TOR-ro-SORE-us)

This horned dinosaur had the largest skull of any land animal ever. It was a massive 8.5 feet (2.6 m) long. Its enormous neck frill was made of a bone shield with large holes in it to lighten its weight—though its skin would have made the shield look solid.

Tt

Triceratops

(try-SER-ah-tops)

This is the best-known of the horned dinosaurs, with dozens of fossilized skeletons found. It grew to 30 feet (9 m) long and may have weighed over 5 tons—as much as a truck! *Triceratops* had three sharp horns growing from its face, and a frill of solid bone grew back from its skull to protect its neck. It is likely that *Triceratops* lived in herds.

FACT...FACT...FACT

Although it was a massive creature, the skeleton of *Triceratops* shows that it was descended from a lively two-legged ancestor. Its hind legs were much longer than its front legs, and its tail would originally have been large enough to balance the weight of the front of the animal when it stood on its hind legs. Many generations of evolution produced the massive *Triceratops* from a smaller creature such as *Psittacosaurus*.

Tylosaurus (TIE-loh-SORE-us)

This 26-foot (8-m) -long sea reptile lived 80 million years ago in the ocean off North America. It had stout, conelike teeth, which it used to crush the shells of various sea animals. Large *Tylosaurus* adults may have attacked other sea reptiles.

Tyrannosaurus

(Tie-RAN-oh-SORE-us)

Tyrannosaurus is the most famous of the large meat-eating dinosaurs. It lived in North America about 70 million years ago and was nearly 50 feet (15 m) long. Its razor-sharp teeth curved backward and measured up to 6 inches (15 cm) long. *Tyrannosaurus* lived at the same time as the horned dinosaurs, such as *Triceratops*, and the hadrosaurs, including *Corythosaurus*. Some scientists think it hunted these large plant-eaters, using its fearsome teeth to kill and tear them apart.

Others think *Tyrannosaurus* moved slowly and so was more likely to feed on the bodies of dinosaurs that had already died. Whether it hunted animals or found dead ones, *Tyrannosaurus* was a powerful and dangerous beast.

A tooth belonging to Tyrannosaurus *shown at actual size!*

Ultrasaurus (ULL-trah-SORE-us)

Ultrasaurus has caused many arguments among scientists. Unfortunately, the fossilized bones found in North America do not make up an entire animal. But there are enough bones to show that this was an unusual beast. *Ultrasaurus* would have been about 115 feet (35 m) long and 26 feet (8 m) tall at the shoulder, with a 40-foot (12-m) -long neck. It would have weighed as much as 20 large elephants! However, some scientists now think the bones really belong to two different animals, not to one. So *Ultrasaurus* may not even have existed!

FACT...

FACT...FACT

The leg bones of *Ultrasaurus* were huge and showed that the complete animal may have weighed up to a staggering 130 tons.

Velociraptor (vee-LOSS-ee-RAP-tor)

This 6.5-foot (2-m) -long dinosaur from Asia lived about 80 million years ago and was related to *Deinonychus*. It hunted prey by gripping the victim with its "hands" and kicking it to death with the large claws on its hind feet. A fossil has been found of a *Velociraptor* and a *Protoceratops* joined together—they killed each other. The *Velociraptor* was kicking the *Protoceratops*, which responded by biting the chest of the hunter.

Wuerhosaurus

(WARE-row-SORE-us)

This stegosaur lived about 120 million years ago in China. It was about 20 feet (6 m) long and had small bony plates along its back. *Wuerhosaurus* was one of the very last stegosaurs to survive, as most had died out millions of years earlier. It is also very rare. Scientists have only found two incomplete skeletons, so its appearance shown here is mostly guesswork.

Xenotarsosaurus

(ZEE-noh-TAR-soh-SORE-us)

This odd hunter was found in Argentina in 1986, and so far only the hind legs and part of a backbone have been discovered. Its name means "strange ankle reptile" and was given to this dinosaur because the ankles of its hind legs were unlike those of any other hunting dinosaur.

Yangchuanosaurus

(YANG-chew-ann-oh-SORE-us)
As the largest hunting dinosaur of its time in Asia, *Yangchuanosaurus* grew to about 30 feet (9 m) long. It lived some 150 million years ago and was armed with very powerful jaws, which could open wider than those of most hunting dinosaurs. Its jaws were filled with very sharp, daggerlike fangs for biting its prey.

Zephyrosaurus

(zeh-FUR-oh-SORE-us)
Zephyrosaurus lived about 110 million years ago in North America. It seems to have been related to *Hypsilophodon*. Like that dinosaur, *Zephyrosaurus* was about 6.5 feet (2 m) long and could run quickly on its hind legs. It ate plants, which it could chew thoroughly with its ridged teeth before swallowing.

Glossary

Ankylosaur A family of dinosaurs with heavy bone armor covering their back and head. Most had a large club on the end of their tail. *Ankylosaurus* and *Talarurus* were both ankylosaurs.

Carnosaur A family of meat-eating dinosaurs. These large creatures had powerful jaws and three-clawed front legs. They were numerous in the Jurassic and Cretaceous Periods. *Megalosaurus* and *Spinosaurus* were both carnosaurs.

Ceratopsian Also known as horned dinosaurs. A family of dinosaurs, most of which walked on all four legs. They had large, sharp horns growing from their skull, and a frill pointing backward over their neck. Ceratopsians lived in Asia and North America in the later Cretaceous Period.

Coelurosaur A family of small, meat-eating dinosaurs that could run fast on their hind legs.

Cold-blooded An animal, like a reptile, that cannot control its body temperature to keep it constant.

Cretaceous A period of Earth's history that began about 135 million years ago and ended about 64 million years ago. This was the last period of the Mesozoic Era, the time of the dinosaurs.

Dinosaur A large group of reptiles that became extinct about 64 million years ago. Dinosaurs can be recognized by details in their skull and hipbones. Dinosaurs lived only on the land; none were adapted for flight or swimming. Scientists divide dinosaurs into two large groups and many families. The two large groups are saurischian and ornithischian.

Dromaeosaurs A group of fast, agile hunting dinosaurs with large, sharp claws on their hind legs. They lived during the Cretaceous Period.

Extinction When a group of animals or plants die out of existence.

Fabrosaurids These were among the earliest plant-eating dinosaurs. They were small dinosaurs that could walk on four legs or run on two. Only partial fossils have been found, so scientists are still unclear about how these dinosaurs are related to each other.

Fossil A bone, leaf, or other remnant of an animal or plant that has been preserved in ancient rocks. Generally the remains have been replaced by minerals and are very hard and heavy.

Hadrosaur Also known as duck-billed. A family of dinosaurs consisting of large plant-eaters that walked mainly on their hind legs. The different species all had broad, ducklike bills at the front of their mouth and many teeth at the rear. Some had bone crests on their head.

Hypsilophodontids This group of plant-eating dinosaurs lived in the late Jurassic and Cretaceous Periods. They could run very quickly and may have lived in herds on open plains.

Ichthyosaur A family of reptiles adapted to life in the ocean. These reptiles looked like fish, but they breathed air and gave birth to live young instead of laying eggs.

Iguanodontids These plant-eating dinosaurs lived in Europe, Africa, and North America during the Cretaceous Period. They walked on two legs and had sharp spiked thumbs.

Jurassic A period of Earth's history that began about 190 million years ago and ended about 135 million years ago. This was the middle period of the Mesozoic Era, the time of the dinosaurs.

Glossary

Nodosaurs A group of dinosaurs with bone armor over their back and head. They were similar to ankylosaurs, except that they did not have a bone club on the end of their tail.

Ornithischian One of the two large divisions within the dinosaur group. Ornithischian dinosaurs had hips shaped like those of modern birds. They were all plant-eaters and included many different types of dinosaur.

Ornithomimid Also known as ostrich dinosaurs. A family of dinosaurs that looked similar to modern ostriches, but with a long tail.

Pachycephalosaurs Also known as bone-headed dinosaurs. A family of plant-eating dinosaurs that had a very thick bone at the top of their skull.

Permian A period in Earth's history that began about 280 million years ago and ended about 225 million years ago. It came just before the era of the dinosaurs.

Plesiosaurs A family of ocean-dwelling reptiles that lived in the Jurassic and Cretaceous Periods.

Prey An animal hunted or captured for food.

Prosauropod A family of plant-eating dinosaurs that lived during the Triassic and early Jurassic Periods. They had long necks and may have been the ancestors of the sauropods.

Pterodactyl A family of pterosaurs. These flying reptiles had very short tails and long, flexible necks.

Pterosaur A large group of flying reptiles. These were not dinosaurs but a special group of reptiles that evolved wings. Each wing was a flap of tough skin stretched between the reptile's body and a very long fourth finger.

Rhamphorhyncoid A family of pterosaurs. These flying reptiles all had long tails with a small rudder at the end.

Saurischian One of the two large divisions within the dinosaur group. Saurischian dinosaurs had hips shaped like those of modern reptiles. They included all the meat-eating dinosaurs as well as the sauropods and prosauropods.

Sauropod A family of plant-eating dinosaurs with long necks and heads. Sauropods included the largest dinosaurs, such as *Ultrasaurus* and *Seismosaurus*.

Stegosaurs A family of plant-eating dinosaurs that had spikes and plates of bone growing out of their back and tail. *Stegosaurus* and *Kentrosaurus* were both stegosaurs.

Theropods Theropod means "beast foot." It is used to describe a group of different types of meat-eating dinosaurs, including tyrannosaurs, dromaeosaurs, and coelurosaurs.

Therapsids A family of reptiles that lived during the Permian, Triassic, and Jurassic Periods. One type of therapsid evolved into mammals.

Triassic A period of Earth's history that began about 225 million years ago and ended about 190 million years ago. This was the first period of the Mesozoic Era, the time of the dinosaurs.

Warm-blooded An animal that can keep its body temperature to a set level.

Wingspan The distance between the wing tips on a bird or flying reptile when the wings are stretched out.

Index

Index